Evensong for Shadows

Evensong for Shadows

Poems

SHANNA POWLUS WHEELER

RESOURCE *Publications* • Eugene, Oregon

EVENSONG FOR SHADOWS
Poems

Copyright © 2018 Shanna Powlus Wheeler. All rights reserved. Except for brief quotations in critical publications or reviews, no part of this book may be reproduced in any manner without prior written permission from the publisher. Write: Permissions, Wipf and Stock Publishers, 199 W. 8th Ave., Suite 3, Eugene, OR 97401.

Resource Publications
An Imprint of Wipf and Stock Publishers
199 W. 8th Ave., Suite 3
Eugene, OR 97401

www.wipfandstock.com

PAPERBACK ISBN: 978-1-5326-5722-1
HARDCOVER ISBN: 978-1-5326-5723-8
EBOOK ISBN: 978-1-5326-5724-5

Manufactured in the U.S.A.   10/24/18

Scripture taken from the New King James Version®. Copyright © 1982 Thomas Nelson. Used by permission. All rights reserved.

"Flames Like People," copyright © 2008 *Christian Century*. Reprinted by permission from the January 14, 2008, issue of *Christian Century*.

"¿*Preguntas?*" copyright © 2017 *Christian Century*. Reprinted by permission from the June 6, 2017, issue of *Christian Century*.

To my husband, Drew, in memory of our three who came before

Contents

Acknowledgments | xi

I. Evensong for Shadows
After a Tour of Britain, | 3
C. S. Lewis Grieving | 4
The Widow's Lament in Autumn | 5
What the Widow Wanted to Say to the Bride | 7
Lo & Behold: A Psalm | 8
I Married a Whistler of Old Hymns | 10
Homily: Variation on a Sestina | 11
The Children Lead Worship | 13
Litany for the Highway Patrol | 14
David with the Head of Goliath | 15
Descant on the 23rd Psalm | 16
Late Autumn on Smith's Knob | 17
Doxology with Crow | 18

II. A Choir of Cells
Jacks | 21
Fertility Lullaby | 22
Sweet Vitriol | 24
Migraine with Aura | 26
Red Knot Turning | 28
Anatomy of the Bleeding Heart | 31
Barrel | 33
Winter Garden | 34
No Poems, | 35
Aftercare | 36

Souvenir | 37
At the Writing Center | 39
Rock-a-bye | 41
Thank You Note | 43
Hot Air | 44

III. The Music of the Spheres
Flames Like People | 49
Haiku in Praise of the Water Chestnut | 50
Bur Song | 51
Glowworm: A Gift | 52
Ode | 53
Spectacle on the Susquehanna | 54
Bell Tower Hymn | 56
Marvel | 57
One Grand Walnut | 58
Opossum in Daylight | 60
Mystic Affection | 62
Voice of the Dung Beetle: Myth I | 63
Voice of the Dung Beetle: Myth II | 65
Dream & Myth of Starlings | 67
Search for Origins | 68
Lunar Eclipse | 70
Verse | 71

IV. Ring of Vowel
¿Preguntas? | 75
Paradiddle | 76
Ballad | 78
Calypso: A Dream | 79
Echolalia | 80
"What is *Near*?" | 81
Local Flooding | 82
Being to Beijing | 83
Academic Dishonesty Policy | 84
Cannonball | 86
Selah | 87
Gamâl | 88

Kairos | 89
Milk Chant | 91
Ars Poetica | 92

Notes on Poems | 93

Acknowledgments

The author gratefully acknowledges the following publications where these poems first appeared, sometimes in earlier versions or with different titles:

The American Journal of Nursing: "Aftercare"

Books & Culture: "Ars Poetica"

Christian Century: "Flames Like People" and "¿Preguntas?"

Christianity & Literature: "Lo & Behold: A Psalm," "Homily: Variation on a Sestina," and "Opossum in Daylight"

Crab Orchard Review: "Spectacle on the Susquehanna"

District Lit: "Search for Origins"

The Evansville Review: "Voice of the Dung Beetle: Myth I"

Every Day Poems (Tweetspeak Poetry): "Voice of the Dung Beetle: Myth II," "Thank You Note," and "Being to Beijing"

First Things: "Academic Dishonesty Policy"

Imago Dei: Poems from Christianity & Literature. Ed. Jill Paláez Baumgaertner. Abilene Christian University Press, 2012: "Opossum in Daylight"

Literary Mama (Birthing the Mother Writer column): "No Poems,"

Mezzo Cammin: "Haiku in Praise of the Water Chestnut," "Doxology with Crow," "Jacks," "Marvel," and "One Grand Walnut"

Mom Egg Review: "Mystic Affection" and "Milk Chant"

Mothers Always Write: "Local Flooding," "*Gamâl*," "Kairos," and "What is Near?"

The New Formalist: "Cannonball"

Acknowledgments

North American Review: "Bur Song"

The Penwood Review: "David with the Head of Goliath" and "Paradiddle"

Relief: "I Married a Whistler of Old Hymns"

Ruminate: "The Widow's Lament in Autumn," "Winter Garden," and "C. S. Lewis Grieving"

Time of Singing: "Bell Tower Hymn"

Tributaries: 50 Years of Susquehanna Literary Magazines. Ed. Gary Fincke. Writers Institute at Susquehanna University, 2014: "Red Knot Turning"

Vineyards: "After a Tour of Britain," and "Descant on the 23rd Psalm"

Watershed: "Late Autumn on Smith's Knob," "Barrel," and "Lunar Eclipse"

The following poems were also published in the chapbook *Lo & Behold* (Finishing Line Press, 2009): "Spectacle on the Susquehanna," "Flames Like People," "Haiku in Praise of the Water Chestnut," "Bur Song," "Marvel," "One Grand Walnut," "Doxology with Crow," "Lo & Behold: A Psalm," "I Married a Whistler of Old Hymns," "Voice of the Dung Beetle: Myth I," "The Widow's Lament in Autumn," "What the Widow Wanted to Say to the Bride," "Opossum in Daylight," "Homily: Variation on a Sestina," "Litany for the Highway Patrol," "Jacks," "Calypso: A Dream," "Being to Beijing," "Thank You Note," "Hot Air," and "Barrel."

Many thanks to the people and institutions that influenced this body of work over the years: Gary Fincke, Karen Holmberg, and the Writers Institute at Susquehanna University—for teaching me the craft and joy of making poems; Robin Becker, Julia Spicher Kasdorf, C. S. Giscombe, and the MFA program in creative writing at Penn State University—for maturing me as a poet and preparing me for a career in higher education; Sascha Feinstein in the English Department at Lycoming College—for welcoming me into a workshop that shaped many of these poems; my former students Bridget Bellmore Carmeci and Krysta Corliss—for teaching me in return; Alexis Czencz Belluzzi—for friendship and insight; fellow writing center directors Deirdre O'Connor and Julie L. Moore—for feedback and encouragement; the faculty writing group at Lycoming College—for the goal-setting and accountability that made all the difference; Marjorie Maddox Hafer—for mentorship at the intersection of faith and art; and my family—for love, support, and many unintentional poem prompts. You are all written into these pages.

I. Evensong for Shadows

After a Tour of Britain,

I dream of nameless ruined abbeys,
naves without roofs
like Holyrood in Edinburgh,

whose great glassless window still rises
behind the Queen's house
like a dreamcatcher—

whose sharp columns
and walls of arches pierce the fog
like a rib cage.

And through the sacred, crumbling space
walks a nameless child
like the one I lost, but older,
or the one I haven't yet conceived.

She strolls the nave's length,
crosses a stone coffin
like a bridge.

At sunset she holds evensong
for shadows; she hums
like an organ pipe.

All night she climbs the mossy stairwells
or waits in dark alcoves
like an unlit lamp.

C. S. Lewis Grieving

> After his published journal, *A Grief Observed* (1961)

        She is dead. The fact
should be as simple
as the sentence I've wrung out of my hand.
        I look at the night sky:
The vast space between stars
and invisible time splashing itself as light
are more certain.
        If I could search the universe
as I would ferret Chaucer from my bookcase,
I would not find her.
        My lover, dead—imponderable comet
with God, fizzing brightly in His presence,
and *like* God, because I cannot see,
cannot recall, the face I have loved
from all angles.
        Her many eyes, noses, mouths!
Her features shifted like her sons' agile limbs
in a playground game:
jackknife reversals of elbows and knees,
and below, the shadows
morphing the geometry of their play.
        She had whole faces
I cannot reassemble now; the endless combinations
cancel each other, so I am left
with no face to remember in love.
This is the tragedy of memory.
        But her voice—her voice
is a clear treble fringed along my weeping.
This is the song of memory.

The Widow's Lament in Autumn

After William Carlos Williams

The box elder bug creeps
from my yard
toward this house,
pushes in like sorrow
through cracks
in doors and windows,
comes to winter in
as the year's light
and warmth run out.
    I watch the black bug
red-flame like a maple leaf
with each clumsy flight
from sill to ceiling.
    I can only crush so many,
one body swathed
in each of a dozen tissues
piled in the waste basket.
    How fickle they are;
once inside they cling
to the sunny window,
looking out
with an insect longing.
    Oh first frost, come soon,
for though I once loved
how the box elder carries
its black-red wings
like a tribal mask
up a window's trim,
I cannot live with it now.
    I have worn enough black;
I can no longer brightly paint

my un-kissed lips.
    It's enough
to winter in
with my own
cold, colorless body.

What the Widow Wanted to Say to the Bride

You should know, you never know
if or when he'll widow you.

Poor widow-me, poor widow-you
someday. You'll see; he'll smirk

in his last picture. Years now
but my closets still smell of him,

a sweet-sour musk. His white suit
a silent "Moonlight Serenade."

Door hinges whistle "Bye Bye
Blackbird" like a dirge. So I moan

of loneliness, pester like a moth
your happy light. Get over it.

You'll never get over widowhood.
I didn't need to tell you.

Hear it? A lone gray dove sings
wi-dow-dow-dow on every wire.

Lo & Behold: A Psalm

After the oral story of Valerie Cook

Newly married and poor, I had run out of food;
    I woke to poverty as to a morning storm.

I fell to my knees before the open freezer door,
      upon the pantry floor below creaking cupboard latches,
    praying to God with each weak plunge.

I cried and waited the morning long.

Lo and behold, at midday, dinner fluttered into the yard:
    a ring neck pheasant so beautiful I saw treasure before I saw food.

The sun set down copper and rubies on its chest,
    rose yellow on either speckled side.

The sky rested blue on rump and wing,
    snow clung round the neck,
    and grass hid its emeralds in the dark head feathers.

Each bead eye pinned down a waddle red as the unseen dinner-heart.

Watching from a window, I woke from this trance of color,
    as if God prodded me with an almighty finger.

I ran for the gun, knowing I had to shoot the bird,
    stunning jewel in God's eye.

The pheasant knew itself an offering,
    knelt down in the crosshairs.

I had to shoot it,
>	because God heard my cry and gave it to me.

When the bullet fast-nested in the bird's plush,
>	I heard in the gun's aftershock, a faint chirp:
>	the bird's song of forgiveness.

Until I plucked the last iridescent feather,
>	until the bird lay naked, bumpy,
>	I scorned myself and the cooling metal of the gun.

But God had loved me with the bird.
>	Lo and behold, I would love Him more.

Praise be to God, whose blessings arrive so richly adorned,
>	that we ache, first with a sweet ache,
>	and then with love.

>	Psalm 138:3

I Married a Whistler of Old Hymns

Tonight "Love Lifted Me"
rings through the hallway. The cat's black-tipped ears
swivel on the chorus—each high *love*
and the notes tumbling after.
        The melody repeats like the tide
but does not weary me, the listener
who cannot whistle, who scrubs dishes
while the whistler carries buckets of coal
from garage to stove.
        This winter night, what cheer
his o-ringed lips offer me;
his embouchure and clear trill lift me
from work-day billows, all my frothy fears
like a daily grace, a hand
like His hand.

Homily: Variation on a Sestina

> In July 2005, an eight-foot-long beehive was removed
> from the rafters of Saint Mark's United Church of Christ
> in Clarion County, PA.

Brothers and sisters of Saint Mark's, church of honey,
of walls glistening gold: There goes your wet kingdom of bees.
Tell me, these seven years have you heard a low buzz,
steady drone beneath the organ's boom and trill as you'd sing
the old songs? When a stray bee wandered through the church
sanctuary during prayer, did you deem it curse or blessing?

And the vast honeycombs—curse or blessing—
stuffing the rafters like the ribs of a fatted calf? Honey,
remember, flavored the manna God gave his people. O church
of rich blessings disguised as a million bees!
The manna fell, remember, like coriander, singing
down with dew. They had to grind and bake it. O buzz,

sweet damage, the many failed fumigations, the resurgent buzz!
But you've read of the Promised Land's syrupy blessing,
how honey flowed from Canaan's rocks. Now loud-sing
the hymn "Honey in the Rock," smiling at the last drips of honey
down the sanctuary walls. Ask, as the drone of bees
quiets, *Have you tasted that the Lord is gracious?* O church,

remember Solomon's wedding song when the church
gathers to scrub the walls, to gut and drywall—all buzzing
ceased, the kingdom hive scraped from the rafters, the loose bees
scattered. Remember Solomon's compliments, blessings:
*Thy lips, O my spouse, drop as the honeycomb: honey
and milk are under thy tongue.* Church of the miracle hive, sing

of the honey spurting from your walls as from rock, sing
of your seven-year blessing of bees.
O church, praise the buzz with every pipe of the organ.

The Children Lead Worship

At the sound of *holy*
        a choir of hands rises,
                each pair pressed in prayer—
        each a small fish
surfacing to kiss air—
        while wrists undulate
                like ripples of incense.
        Is this how holy moves?
Is this the current of Spirit
        through unclean hands
                made clean by His?

Litany for the Highway Patrol

Praise the cruiser's white length, rack of lights.
Praise its thick-letter decal, insignia, bold stripe horizontal.
Praise the shock when the hill ducks down,
      when the concrete beam of an overpass glides by.

Praise how the cruiser straddles a grassy median.
Praise its stealth,
      how we never catch its slow roll behind fence, bush, sign.
Praise the cruiser poised on a ramp's sloping side,
      how the parking brake stays gravity.

Praise the wide nose of the speed gun, gauge of our transgression,
      and slung out a window gripping it, the khaki arm.
Praise the gloved trigger finger.
Praise the keen eyes under felt-hat shadow.

Praise the quick light-up and lurch, the bright privilege,
      each bulb revolving: blue, red, shrieks of silver.
Praise the wild-flash-chastisement in the speeder's rearview mirror.
Praise the cruiser's halting power,
      how the speeder quick-humbles.
Praise the trooper's bend-down inquiry, rebuke of miles per hour.

Praise the highway patrol;
      we are all demons speeding past limits.

David with the Head of Goliath

> Girolamo Forabosco (1670)
> Palmer Museum of Art, Penn State University

In this nook of old master oils,
young David keeps his balance, holds
the huge head atop his shoulder,

pulls a tuft of the Philistine's black hair.
I flinch at the upside-down grimace
of thick tongue and shadow.

I know how David later plunged
from righteousness, let his eye roll
down the curves of Bathsheba's body.

How burdensome the ghastly head:
Even then, anointed and victorious,
David carried his guilt toward Jerusalem.

The scarlet of the stone-wound
matches the scarlet of the cloak
wrapped around his shoulders.

I look long at David's dark eyes
like marbles, cast downward,
impossibly serene.

The bright bulbs overhead warm me
like forgiveness, like the invisible,
pardoning hand of grace.

Descant on the 23rd Psalm

Flock out blotching the hill like low clouds:
        Praise your shepherd, who gives you green fields of clover.

Sheep upturned in a furrow, belly-up under cloud shadow:
        Your shepherd will find you.

Though your body bloats till your legs prod the air like weeds,
        do not fear death.

All but your shepherd would think you long dead,
        you stiff, fog-eyed sheep.

He will kneel beside you, knowing you cannot breathe,
        and roll you from the furrow.

He will knead your belly, massage loose your joints;
        you will blink from his comfort.

He will restore you to your feet;
        though your legs shake, he will steady you.

He will lead you home;
        you will walk light as a cloud.

Praise the shepherd, O sheep, and rejoice,
        for he comes soon.

Look for the crook of his staff bounding over the field.

Late Autumn on Smith's Knob

> Loyalsock State Forest, PA

Half the hike up, the terrain nearly levels.
No lookout or vantage yet, but a sense of altitude,
even as our knees bend less with each step,
as our breathing slows and quiets.

The atmosphere at eye level: yellow leaves
suspended, afloat but for the limbs
of young trees, their slight structures
emerging later, once the awe has aged.

At our feet, yellow piles spaced every ten yards
or so, the trail scraped flat between.
We imagine the hunter dragging the limp body
of the hunted only so far before tiring again,

shifting grip, brushing aside leaves with a boot,
and trudging further. Such labor
paid the debt of his kill, we think, as a vista
of ridges and water-carved valleys opens.

What tribute—beyond our sweat gone cold,
beyond pause and exhalation—
might we pay? What can we leave behind
like these plush, bright cairns?

Doxology with Crow

> "*Awe, / awe,* they cry."
> –Donald Platt

For the levity of your full black bulk
high-stepping over snow; for your cloak
of oil, how the sun reveals its gem-spectrum;
for your unfurled wings shimmering: praise Him.

II. A Choir of Cells

Jacks

I play jacks with my mother, impossibly
young as she, seven or eight, spindly,
kneeling on linoleum under dim, orange light.

Between our knob-knees bings the rubber ball;
the jacks chink in quick fists. First to gather all
ten without a double bounce or mishap,

my mother wins. *Always said she was good at jacks*,
I think. I watch her darker hair willow down long
beside mine, see freckles shift with a smirk,

hear her hand clasp jacks: a fist full of molecules like God's.
This tinny jingle of jacks is the jumbled song of me.
In dreams I meet the girl not yet dreaming of me.

Fertility Lullaby

You carried your first pink days
like thin water goblets, glass
ornaments, eggs on a spoon.

You stood naked before a mirror:
Below the ripples of your ribs,
below your navel, a child could nest.

All these years of maturation, look
how you've cringed as your uterus
pumps blood like a second heart.

And now, with your two hearts,
you can't imagine a third—
tiny twitching heart within a heart.

You've heard how tenuous
the first and final months—
nothing guaranteed but pain.

But think how a baby lulls a womb
with a choir of cells splitting in song
hush-a-bye, don't you cry.

How the monthly lurch ceases
still as the trill of a thrush
in a twilight high.

How the body nurtures another,
the bones giving nutrient
a mockingbird.

How inevitably you will love
when you wake you shall have
a child. Love lull you fearless

don't say a word.

Sweet Vitriol

> *First Operation under Ether,* Robert C. Hinckley (1883)

Framed and hung on my dentist's wall is the damage of Eden
reversed: the moment pain drowned in ether. Watch it glisten

in Dr. Morton's inhaler, a glass bowl with a gadget
jutting out like a straight faucet. The boy Abbot

with a tumorous jaw had set his lips around it minutes before,
breathing in deeply, mumbling as he slumped in the chair,

of *dreams, wonderful dreams*—of bodiless visions
spinning down the shore of chemical sleep, where incisions

are lines in sand, or snails, rubicund and drawn on a white birch.
Dr. Warren applies the scalpel to Abbot's neck. No flinch,

no staccato jerk of his small head resting on the pillow.
The spectators in the arena strain to see from the shadows

while the light falls on the heads of the thirteen men huddling
around Dr. Warren, all dressed darkly, long-coated, muttering

as he works the tumor from its numb, veined nest.
Gentlemen, he will say to the crowd in his success,

after he has stitched the incision and Abbot wakes,
bears witness of no pain, only the scalpel's dull scrape

at his jaw, *This is no humbug*—this fluid Raymond Lully
discovered six centuries ago, which he named *sweet vitriol:*

the alchemic fusing of what we have always desired
with the fury we ride, jetting ourselves toward comfort.

Migraine with Aura

Phase 1

Serotonin teems as it shouldn't
so suddenly between brain cells,

this eager molecule of message saying
Blood vessels, pull in your walls,

disturbing my visual cortex,
conceiving the aura.

Phase 2

I go dime-blind, some currency of vision
rubbed away as by a fingertip.

Words disappear in turns across a page.
My mirror image loses an eye.

Not a gaping—the no-eye, then no-nose—
but a fleshy blur, erasure: the preface of aura.

Phase 3

The aura's a crescent moon rising,
moon of re- and re- refracted light,

curvature of tumbling sparks, scythe aglow
with my fury. I lose half a sky of vision

to zigzag turbulence, this vertical smile of ill wishes
of bright blindness: the preface of migraine.

Phase 4

Serotonin swiftly recedes
from intercellular space.

A silent blood rush, a red return
reverses the vessel trauma.

All this, the migraine's push-pull arrival:
the pressure skull-ward, the load laid down.

Red Knot Turning

I find Nana in the basement—
        in the poorly lit
retired dance studio, a forty-year business
        in this house
fortified by stucco and stone—
        stirring her laundry.

She holds a wooden paint stirrer firm
        in her right fist,
lid of the washing machine
        open, gaping.

Fans of water soak the clothes within,
        wetting the Tide
powder from blue-speckled white
        to foam.
She pokes it all down, blending her load
        like dense, chilled soup.

It's late December, two weeks till my first
        surgery, a slight
procedure, but six months since her Whipple,
        the reshuffling

of digestion, how the stomach
        listens to what's left
of the pancreas, how it speaks to enzymes
        and learns a new way
to empty itself.

I ask, *How will it be when I'm under,*
        much like sleeping?
I've never blacked out or fainted
        to awaken

knowing only a prior, uninterrupted
        moment. *Strange?*

How to trust the time you lose,
        how anesthesia
wraps up pain in its obliterating
        sheet, a white

hospital blanket that soaks it up,
        blood taking to gauze
while you're numb in your twilight
        or deep, monitored night.

She answers, *When I was a teenager*
        getting my tonsils out,
they gave me ether; I'll never forget it.
        She raises her fists
to eye level, bends her elbows
        to point outward,

her forearms flattening to a line,
        a white, veined
horizon. *I saw this blood red*
        knot turning

(She grinds fist over fist, wrists
        rotating, knuckles
bumping along palms) *and turning.*
        Her eyes squint
at the memory, now a dark red load,
        a heart spinning

between us in red atmosphere,
        that organ of feeling
anesthesia holds outside the body
        for a time.

Anatomy of the Bleeding Heart

Lamprocapnos spectabilis

Pluck the charm
from its green chain.

Feel at a pinch
this pocketbook's bony goods.

Prod through the flower's modesty,
its heart-shaped encasement.

Tug the exposed toes
dripping like dew, not blood.

Separate the heart's halves. Say
I want these pink lungs

flop-eared like bunnies.
Now the flower lies without cover,

a hanger without a shirt.
Touch the pliable frame

of arcs white as bone.
Say *I want to hang my skin*

from these cool shoulder blades,
my hips from this delicate pelvis.

Pull apart the arcs, leaving
two slippers sole to sole

with frills and gills
of royal silk. Say

*I'll wear them
as more ornamental clavicles,*

*less rigid jawbones,
or more exquisite brows.*

Divide the soles to find
the smooth wand within

like a porcelain drumstick,
conductor's baton.

Say *O lovely spine,
be my sensory column*

*of soft but indestructible ivory,
my body's wire of touch.*

*O bleeding heart, give me
all your fragrant anatomy.*

Barrel

> Lock Haven, PA

From this bench cemented to the levee's river walk,
I watch a buoy lean and bob with the current
swift from yesterday's rain.

A dam spans shore to shore
over which the Susquehanna bends and plummets,
then roars to rapids.

Locals have drowned here, have slid over
the smooth shoulder
into the turbine of water below, the body caught
in ceaseless undertow, the body tumbling
out of breath.

Under autumn's morning sunlight,
I watch a blue barrel bounce on the rapids,
having rolled over the dam days ago.

How long will the barrel dance
to the river's burly song, will its fearless plastic
mock the undertow? How long
will the water's arms challenge its fat buoyancy?

How long will I perch in this unsinkable joy?

Winter Garden

Our coal bin full, the yard mottled with leaves
like birds, the wind cutting sunlight, autumn
here, winter coming—but we had a garden
we meant to grow indoors, harvest in spring.
While summer still cheered us with green leaves
and late sunsets, and the garden—still a secret—
seemed firmly rooted, nourished with our hope,
the garden failed, withering in secret.

We've cleared our hidden plot. We mourn and wait.
The days shorten. Morning and evening chill us.
Prayer tills the soil of our winter garden;
hope again turns it.

No Poems,

those few months
my body made yours.
It was enough
to make a heart flicker
first in secret, later
like a grain of rice
on the ultrasound—
to make your fragile sprout
of brain stem and spine,
your toe and finger buds,
the fused lids
of your still-forming eyes.

O the mercy in your brief,
unconscious existence:
You knew only
the peace of darkness,
of silence, and now,
if I can believe it,
only light and song.

No poems
in the months after, either.
Only revisions, the effort
to get it right, to align
and realign words
like cells—
to urge the flame,
spur the song. To finish
the rough work
barely begun.

Aftercare

>For Janet Andrus

At your table of mercy, you fed me watermelon
and warm tapioca fluffed with egg whites.

You gave me an embroidery kit and pillowcase,
that I might stitch flowers into my dreams.

At your table of mercy, I pulled needle and thread
through fabric with ease; I fixed each mis-stitch.

My womb having abandoned its ornate project,
I reclaimed consent with the grip of my hands.

At your table of mercy, I found a pattern for grief.
To make was to mourn what could not be made.

Souvenir

>   For Janet Andrus

Aside from Welsh dragon flags
along the streets of Llangollen,
hand-carved kissing spoons in gift shop windows,
the canal barge tour through sheep pastures
and over the aqueduct spanning the valley,

I remember the sign on the mirror
in the public restroom, how it diagrammed
parts of the hand we seldom scrub: the back,
the palm's plush outer edge, that web
of skin between thumb and index finger—
here we carry scourges, like the swine flu
breaking on British news channels.

Under that sign I washed my hands
with more vigor than ever—
massaged neglected regions of my flesh
with which I had touched Welsh trinkets,
antique tea cups, a Border Collie's friendly head,
and doorknobs to rooms in buildings
older than my own country.

I washed them as you do, retired nurse.
I've watched suds cover your pink skin
like wool, your fingers weaving, braiding water,
palm sliding against palm and bumping over
knuckles, one hand cleansing the other, yet tender,
as you were to your many patients.

Your hands could lift centuries-
old coal stains from Edinburgh's buildings.
Your hands still comfort, still heal
like the warm green waters at Bath,
in which I dipped and swirled my fingers
despite the warning sign.

I offer them to you, these hands
that grazed cathedral walls and castle stone
and cradled London grit.

At the Writing Center

> Lycoming College, Williamsport, PA

She's come to have me *take a look*
at her essay on why she hopes
to transfer from our liberal arts
and study radiography instead.

And like a traitor, I must help her
shape her message—aid and abet
her abandonment of our humanities,
fine arts, social and natural sciences.

I notice vague redundancies,
suggest cuts to leave more room
for specifics. Her reasons appear
trite, unmemorable.

I urge her to write about the technology,
what the x-rays and ultrasounds
allow us to see and know
for the sake of patient care.

As she types new details, the foggy,
shifting images of my own womb
return to mind—each time
the fetal globe pulsed early on,

then not at all soon after. No words
or gestures of comfort came
from the techs, just clinical descriptions
like *collapsed gestational sac.*

I want to tell her the brief stories
of my unborn, whose only portraits
are the black-and-white stills
filed in a cabinet of medical records

like the nameless patients in the waiting room
of her future. What will she say and do
when the rays expose in brilliant white
the personal disasters—

when the waves wash over *products
of conception,* then coldly retreat?
May she take whatever arts we've given her.
May she apply them liberally.

Rock-a-bye

>For Sophia

Not quite two, you sing *O my soul*
to the radio's praise chorus
from your five-point harness car seat.

Will I tell you someday
how the three who came before you
did not live to sing?

And how in dreams
my knees buckled beneath me
every time I carried a child?

I folded, collapsed like a splintered ladder.
The child tumbled out of reach,
disappearing into daylight.

Awake, I was the unstable cradle
on the treetop, a vessel ever
overturning until you.

I grew full—sturdy, steady—
then carried your newborn body
without fear, until I tripped

over the cat, dropped to my knees,
clutched your ribcage with one hand,
slapped the floor with the other.

The dream returned with your face,
with the kiss-shaped birthmark
on your cheek red-blooming, flaring.

I feel its radiance now
against my chest as we rock,
as you sing to my heart of the bough.

Thank You Note

> For Sarah Pierce Reeder

Friend, I hear the wind chime ring, its shifting six-note melody.
The chime's long-legged like you, twirling on occasion, like you.
When I feel inside out, you say, *I spin around.* The day I pulled it
from the box, the chime lay limp as a puppet unstrung, dead-heavy,
the hollow metal bars splayed across my arms. Now it hangs
from a porch rafter singing *Praise be to gravity for these taut strings.*

Hot Air

>For Barbara Jo Powlus

Not my friend, the one who pilots hot air balloons
over south Jersey. I didn't drift over flat farm fields,
spy the Philly skyline to the northwest, the green Atlantic
to the east and south.
      Forgive me, I've stolen your vantage,
the slow rush of ascent like a billow below your sternum.
Now mine, your timid offerings of sweat and stomach tremor
to gravity.
    I nest in the densely weaved basket, wingless
but soon unafraid of wind-sway, sudden shifts in current.
                I just
wanted to put a hot air balloon into a poem—I loved your telling
of how its envelope fat with nothingness
carried you smooth as elation.
          The poem wants for its bare atmosphere
the balloon's bright quilt patterned like a tessellation,
rivaling Joseph's famed coat.
       Oh just me and the pilot
in the balloon in the poem, whose blue sky must extend to fit
our slow float nowhere, whose fields of all shades of green
must multiply row by row.
        One long panoramic look,
and we must descend. My ears pop with each layer of sky
the basket eases through.
      Closer now to land,
to the best part of your trip, what you will never forget,
what the poem saves for its final lines:
              We sink
toward rows of high corn—not a clearing, not yet.
The pilot regulates the heated air
so the balloon slows to a hover above the field.

We glide horizontally, fall a little lower. Some wind, a swifter glide, and the basket grazes the field.
                             I feel and hear
each corn stalk's yellow tassel flick the basket below my feet
just like you said.
                 Oh the poem has no room left
for such joy.

III. The Music of the Spheres

Flames Like People

Thank you, Morgan, preschool prodigy of likenesses.
I hadn't considered my propane heater
so closely, its hot imagery, how, as you declared that winter evening
in my kitchen, munching a chip two-handed
like a squirrel, the heater's line of flames looks like people.
And as your younger sister Ella whirled
in pink britches around the kitchen singing *flames like people,
people dancing*, and as you grinned
at your own brilliance and the brilliant line of half-blue, half-orange folk
you culled up with spark of thought
and vapor of breath, I saw them too, figures swinging hips
with whippy fervor to the beat of ignition.

Born seeking likenesses, each of us. We secure a simile,
like the wild Ella scooped and wrapped
in her father's arms, let it burn to purer metaphor, let it cool
as we celebrate, as we praise our precocity.
Really, we praise the world, we delight in its many
wrought likenesses.

Haiku in Praise of the Water Chestnut

How dull the stir fry
bereft of these white discs, coins.
Dear water chestnut.

Sing between my teeth.
How I love your percussion
as my teeth slice through.

O fresh, fresh tuber.
Eager as a potato,
you sprout if too warm.

Charitable treat.
How kind you are to let me
peel your skin like fruit.

Most steadfast chestnut.
No wok robs your crunch, no boil
can soften your song.

Bur Song

sing the bur
like spur like starburst

sing oh
the bur's hooks and prickles
dry-tangle glue

sing the fruit of ankle weeds
sly seed vessel

the burdock's
grape-oval bur
with tapered spikes

the cocklebur's
needle-stuck strawberry

and oh the many-speared
blueberries of bur grass
bur clover

sing oh the bother of burs

the bane of sheep shearers
woodland trekkers

sing the bur
stubborn traveler

sticky-thumbed
subtle hitchhiker

brute spiny wonder

Glowworm: A Gift

> After William Wordsworth's poem
> "Among all lovely things my Love had been" (1807)

Love, if these woods
far from Wordsworth's
unfurl in bioluminescence,
I'll trek bur-weed paths
at dusk and wait
for one kind glowworm
to light its lamp.

I'll cradle the lime-lit
creature in a leaf,
carry it home to you.
And if it still casts
yellow-green beams,
I'll lay the brilliant ornament
under the lilac, come find you,
lead you as the poet
led his Lucy.

As one body we'll marvel
over the worm's bright body,
take joy in the lightsong,
the radiant hum.

Ode

    For Drew

You see swaths of rain like curtains
miles before drops pelt the roof.

I scan darkening clouds for signs:
Is that a veil of rain above the ridge?

In the woods, you witness the whitetail flash.
On the lake, you catch the green splash of bass

and hear the bullfrog's rusty horn.
I wait for second shows, second calls.

Teach me your supersensory ways—
to observe preemptively, to hear pre-sound.

Spectacle on the Susquehanna

        Lock Haven, PA

From the levee's river walk
I saw three figures walk

like gods atop the water,
march the river's middle water

where no rapids gesture to depth,
not a ripple rats out the depth.

Roving in three directions (up river,
toward the levee, to the far bank of the river)

they meant to awe.
And I watched in awe,

cursed by their spectacle.
They spread wide their spectacle

on the Susquehanna, its water cursed to buttress
their feet like the levee's buttress

of asphalt below mine. But the sun shimmered
as it set, and near their feet the water shimmered

in patches of gold leaf. Stones,
I thought, a mound of stones

must nearly break the surface,
their feet trekking not the surface

but the riverbed, only daring the shallows,
only boasting across the shallows

to the awe of passersby. Half released, I walked
downriver, fool-spirited, gawking back as I walked.

Bell Tower Hymn

       Flemington, PA

Child, as the chipped green seesaw leavens you,
listen to the bell song you rise toward and through:

old hymn "This is My Father's World."
On the hour, the park air resounds;

you breathe in chimes like the sawdust your feet
stir up as you scurry to the super slide and creep

up the steps through the ringing air.
Sliding down, sing *To my listening ears,*

all nature sings. Child, round you rings the music of the spheres.
Hear it? Hum as you pull the sand digger's yellow levers.

Ride the merry-go-round, cling to the metal bars
as the woods and baseball field green-blur.

Oh let the thought of rocks and trees,
skies and seas, rest you, stunned and dizzy,

singing as you leap off
His hand the wonders wrought.

Marvel

Yards from a murmurless creek
grows this crooked cherry
with a zig-zag trunk,
angular as

the lightning bolt that struck it,
snapped its trunk nearly off,
thus the zag, the sharp
sag, the steep jut

downward. Yet the cherry lived,
mending its fracture, now
an arthritic joint,
bulbous and thick.

Livid then, the cherry grew
up against the droop, thus
the trunk's second joint,
the zig—it looks

just like a human elbow,
and the whole double-kink
trunk, like an arm bent
to wrestle air.

One Grand Walnut

> For Louise Johnson and Bill Raco

I left it, one grand walnut now rooted deep
in my hundred-acre alfalfa field.
I don't remember why—a spot of shade
in summer maybe—nothing to do with art.
But once every season, camera in hand,
a neighbor stands in the field, far enough
away to capture the perfect globe
of branches. He eyes the walnut between shots
as if waiting for wind to flip the leaves
like the wings of restless birds, or the sun
to light the dense network like the burning bush.
He gave me a gift of three framed shots.
The walnut in winter: an eerie nest, gray sky.
Decked in summer's greenery, the walnut leans
in a yellow breeze. Harvest: now I see
the walnut orange and round as a pumpkin.
My kitchen window frames the tree each day;
I never noticed till his watchful stance,
the camera lifted to his eye, and these
pictures of a tree always just a tree
firm in the field, left to burrow roots
and broaden branches skyward. Growth, I saw,
not grandiosity, my eyes on sprays
of cow's milk, my hands powdered with feed.
I've lived too close to the land, seeing use
and yield. I now look twice at eager sprouts
of alfalfa, each bony calf, each crooked
line of leg. My square-bodied cows are black
and white photographs. The strutting rooster

embodies sunset and autumn. My eyes:
a camera. All of it art—these acres,
these animals, the walnut that nods to me.

Opossum in Daylight

Gray baby, we caught you
in a Havahart cage below the front step.

    O dew-tipped hair

Was it you
    O spool of spun silver
digging holes in the lawn?

    O ghost face

We twirled your cage to have a look at you.

    O razor leer
    O low hiss

We shut you
    O night liver, O moon lover
into the trunk's dark
and drove to the woods.

We lowered the cage, eased open
both doors, but
    O five-fingered grip, O rope-tail curled around metal
you wouldn't move.

So we shook loose your hold
till you slid stiff as death to the dirt.

    O furred fear
    O still shiverer

Nocturnal wanderer, we left you stunned
by sunlight,
    O pound of shock
by our eyes bright as sky.

    O little body electric

Mystic Affection

When the light shifted over my face, I woke to find you
wandering the hall and whispered, *It was the moon,*

because you were confused by dreams. *Come back to bed,*
where we drifted to our separate darknesses, while our child,

who has begun to acquaint the painted orbs and crescents
in her thick-paged books with their bright referent,

slept in her crib across the hall. *Moon, moon!* she cries
when she spots it through a window. Searching the sky

in daylight, she sees against the blue its slight print.
When it hides behind clouds, she opens books, finds it

gracing brush-stroked skies or masquerading
as the gray underside of a mallard duck's wing.

She points to the roused bird, *O moon,* then kisses the page.

Voice of the Dung Beetle: Myth I

    In Africa, I asked the moon
to marry me.

    O moon, my onyx body shines
a greenish-blue

    in your full light. O find me rare—
viridian—

    as jade. My love, fall near to me
tonight, all nights.

    I'll hold you in my arching arms,
my armored arms.

    The moon did not reply at first;
I lurched, I lunged.

    I dug my head in sand for shame,
for foolishness.

    Just then the moon said, *If you swear*
to me you'll sweep

    the earth—you'll clean, unsully it—
I'll marry you.

    And so I swore by love, by stars,
I'd spend my days

    half perched, my legs embracing dung
I've hugged to spheres—

       that round moon shape I laud. I roll
and bury, shape

       and roll and bury, on and on:
Love's rearward walk.

Voice of the Dung Beetle: Myth II

        In Egypt, I am Kheper, god
in beetle form.

        My mundane work—such drudgery—
elicits awe.

        They deify this dung-dulled back,
these daggered feet

        that pat and spin foul spheres, adept
as spider legs,

        which wrap and shape the stunned to balls,
to chrysalides

        of death. But spun up in my spheres
is larval life.

        They do not know I drop the dung
in burrows, leave,

        begin the work again. In time,
when beetles rise

        from sand—a crop that scurries, root-
less harvest, hard

        and rigid-armored—Egypt kneels
in foolish praise.

        To them, we scarabs self-create,
and like Khepri,

        our namesake god, who rolls the sun
across the sky,

        we trace horizons with our spheres
and (true) create our days.

Dream & Myth of Starlings

In a cathedral of pin oak branches,
Zacchaeus perches, apple in hand.

The wind's children sing evensong—
old ballad of this man, in whose palm

the apple splits into perfect halves,
from which a star rises, swells,

bursts in a rustle of frantic wings.
I wake to a shrill chorus of starlings.

From my window, I watch the oak shiver—
leaves or wings? Now a swarm skyward:

a black rush back to the star, to the seed
of the apple—back to the mouth of God.

Search for Origins

August 2001

Bring a piece of Sun to Earth,
NASA says, abridging astrophysics.
That'll use up decades worth of Petri dishes.
That'll grant the laboratories light
years of microscopic scrutiny of
hydrogen and helium,
nameless ions, purest isotopes.
That'll pay the debt of launch,
orbit at the point of equal gravity between
Earth and Sun, the flight back home, released
parachute, the mid-air snatch
via helicopter (simulated and rehearsed).
That'll tell us how the planets sprung
out of solar nebula, a cloud of ice,
swirling gas and dust;
why the Earth has welcomed life;
why no atmosphere shrouds Mercury;
why thick clouds of poison cloak
Venus; what that cloud—born from collapse,
death of stars, their cast off, shucked
particles—contained.

November 2001

Genesis: the cargo ship of solar wind;
vehicle of Search for Origins;
wristwatch-shaped robotic craft with
twenty-two-foot solar paneled wings
sized to wrap a Titan's wrist;
capsule like a pocket-watch with latch

set to open at the point of balance,
bloom, unfurl collector arrays,
disks designed to catch the solar wind
via hexagonal tiles of gold,
diamond, sapphire, silicon:
precious, manmade, gleaming honeycombs.

September 2004

Glitch of parachute. The capsule pierces
Utah's desert. Tiles shatter, glitter scatters.
NASA gathers up the shards.
Scientists say this'll set us back.
Even so, the science left—the still-pure
particles of Sun like grains of salt, a dash—
promises a century's research,
astrophysicists' delight, tactile fodder for the search.

Lunar Eclipse

> February 20, 2008
> Lycoming College, Williamsport, PA

Tonight a mustached black man
impersonates King, recites the famed
dream speech before a sparse crowd.
His spot-on howl and refrain crescendo
through the science lecture hall.
Have we realized the dream? he asks.

Outside, the astronomy professors shiver
around a silver telescope on wheels,
hoping the clouds disperse.
The moon already bathes in the umbra,
but they can't see it yet—the change in hue
to orange or red, brown or gray.

If the clouds clear before midnight,
before the moon fully casts the skin of shadow,
what will the moon in metamorphosis
tell them? What will they discern
from the moon's unpredictable hue
about where we should go from here?

Verse

A line turns at the edge of thought and sense
like the swivel of a tractor in a field.
A thought may change the mind like repentance,
the choice to turn around, go back—to yield.
But without will, the downy seeds disperse
from dandelions, caught in whirls of wind.
And the earth (hear it?) moans; it can't reverse
its orbit, break ellipse, or cease to spin—
a speck, a mere blue glint, in the churn
of galaxies in space. The universe:
one infinite turn. What hope of return
for matter or mind? No line of verse
can stir like Scripture—only the very voice
of God can still all turning, reverse all choice.

IV. Ring of Vowel

¿Preguntas?

> Only 1% of women miscarry three
> or more times. In 50–75% of these cases,
> no medical cause can be found.
> —The American College of Obstetricians
>   and Gynecologists (2016)

At first a mistake, now a willful, recurrent error:
    I mistranslate the Spanish

on medicine labels to mean "Pregnant?"
    though it means "Questions?"

Yes, I'm pregnant with questions. The words equate
    no matter the language.

I've sown flesh of my flesh but reaped only mystery
    with its low fog of grief.

An irony of fruitfulness: I bear questions like choice figs
    while answers hide

like Nathanael under the branches. God, you see through,
    but do not translate.

I call your number in the morning; you call back
    with psalms, David crying

"Why?" in one breath and singing wonders
    in another.

Paradiddle

Katia, bless her,
how she startled
the prayer ring,
women gathered
with heads low-bowed,
when her English,
thick-accented,
halting, lilting,
thrummed smooth as balm
to Portuguese.
With ease of tongue
what numberless
supplications
rose to heaven
on those quick-spun
syllables like
paradiddle
beats on a snare.
She astonished
us to worship.
Each transfigured
request was mine.
And so I knew
she prayed for me,
Katia, bless her,
then cupped my knee,
tightening grip
with each long ring
of vowel, each
sharp consonant.
My slight requests
Katia uttered,
and so lifted

my soul to God,
sing-speaking
in angelic
tongue, so it seemed,
and in cadence
with choruses
wrought for heaven.

Ballad

> "Look what they gived us,
> and we didn't even want it!"
>
> —The author, age 3

About the time I pinched the tail—
two fingers lifting a stiffened mass
of matted mouse, its fur
blackened from feline spit—

my tongue experimented with tense,
referred to three years done: my past.
I gave to a young yesterday
what was to me the proper ending, -ed.

Contractions were intrinsic trimmings
to my verbal code—instinctual crunch,
apostrophe's claw scratching space
above the dropped vowel.

We scurry to simplify; time's lost
in lengthened syntax. So sure
of shortcut, we don't want
expired mice, a wasted past.

Calypso: A Dream

The sloop John B, sea-worn, sways
        in Nassau harbor, bearded with barnacles, rocked by waves
and the ruckus on board.

I mourn for the boy who may never go home,
        young Odysseus, who cries
to his grandfather, to the constable and sheriff, to let him go home.

Drunk, the first mate smashes the cargo.
        The cook throws the boy's grits overboard, picks a fight.
The captain's lost ashore.

All night the boy squints seaward through his black eye.
        He sings only
of brokenness. The sun never rises.

I hear strums of guitar,
        my father and I singing *Hoist up the John B's sail.*
See how the mainsail sets.

I wake to the memory: our collapsible metal music stand, the guitar
        saddling my father's crossed leg,
and from our lips the boy's plea: *Call for the captain ashore.*

Barely literate, I had loved how *sloop*
        slid off my curl of tongue, the patter of one-beat words,
string upon string.

I understood the longing for home; I grieved for the boy even as
        the nonsense syllables
played calypso on the drum of my ear.

Echolalia

Years after scrawling the unfamiliar word
on this scrap of paper now falling
from the pocket of an old coat,

I hear my expressions repeated
in toddler-speak: tongue-slurred
sound bites from my child's lips.

Reading to her, I annotate stories,
direct her ears and eyes to details in corners
of pages or hidden in spines:

This is the car waiting for Little Sal
and her mother at the bottom
of Blueberry Hill. *Iss-is da ca.*

Tonight, fish and fowl, animals wild
and tame, swarm the pages
of an illustrated creation story.

We find Adam and Eve (*Ad-neev*)
standing amidst bushes. *They're naked—
naked bodies—but they don't mind.*

Dun mine. We talk of bath time
and how just after, Daddy chases her wet curls
through the house. We turn the page:

The first man and woman sit facing each other
at sunset. *Naked bodies,* she echo-speaks,
her fingers grazing their knees and elbows like ferns.

"What is *Near*?"

> –Sophia, age 3

She waits in the liminal space of curiosity
while I secure the harness of her car seat.

She brings Ella's croon of nearness to mind
as her eyes drift past me to the pale moon.

In answer, I press my cheek to hers
and whisper, *This, this is near—*

a quiet thrill, a warm delight of skin on skin
not reserved for lovers, oh no; children

and parents are granted the right of nearness.
A prompt of sweet conversation—the dearest

question—daughter, draws me to you,
oh you, my wildest dream come true.

Local Flooding

> Montoursville, PA

The fascination of the day, the word
cutting a groove in my daughter's mind
like urgent rainwater: flood—

*when it rains and rains and rains
and water rises and rises,* she says
with a flourish of lips and arms
after watching a YouTube montage—
Pennsylvania towns like Bloomsburg
and Hershey drowning in September, 2011.

You were a baby, I tell her,
*so you don't remember your stroller ride
down muddy Broad Street,*
when we gawked at ruined homes
while she napped to the drone
of Shop-Vacs and water pumps.

Our town flooded? she asks and waits.
A speck of Ark floats in each wide blue eye.

Being to Beijing

She goes by Abby, though her Chinese name,
Wanjing, still flits its wings among the roll
of this mostly white composition class.
She writes of the weather in Beijing, how
the moment you hear thunder, *already
rain drops on face, with no time to pull out
umbrella*. I hesitate to edit-in
the modifiers lost in translation.

Look: she does not clutter the portrait.
She makes no waste of this language strange
to her tongue. So I hear clearly, in her sparse
sentences, longing for Beijing. It builds,
and in the final paragraph, she meant
to type *being*, but *Beijing* rings instead.

Academic Dishonesty Policy

Don't borrow another's thought
without citation. Don't filch
another writer's diction,
assuming I'm deaf to style
and tone—elements I teach.
Remember, if you Google,
copy, paste, I will follow
the crumbs, find your swiped intro,
patchwork body paragraphs.
I will expose each captive,
orphaned sentence. Why abduct?
So easy to give credit
than to discredit yourself,
even if your appendix,
little worm of an organ,
just gave you three weeks' trouble
and a backlog of schoolwork—
like Pranav, the first student
of mine to steal swaths of text
from unacknowledged sources.
His forced act of penitence:
new essay, open topic.
This is not some parable
I've devised. I couldn't build
irony to this degree:
He chose the topic karma.
Believers blame their actions,
not God, for their misfortune,
he wrote, then quoted Buddha:
According to the seed that's
sown, so is the fruit you reap—

an echo of Galatians.
I wrote *F = Bad Fruit*
as my only end comment.

Cannonball

       For Janet Andrus

What you saw on your walk down Vesper Street,
as you passed below a young maple tree:
First the branches launched a blackbird skyward
like a cannonball. Then a thump—a bird,
a starling at your feet, dust like gun smoke
rising, the poor bird dead and dusky black.
I wonder: Was this mere coincidence
or feathered carnage, a bird murder—hence,
the blackbird's wild escape, stunt vertical
in ice-dry air? No, back to *cannonball*,
whose synonyms include *note, epistle,
dispatch*. Then could it be the starling's soul
shot itself heavenward as a blackbird?
Ah, cannonball—both blackbird and this dirge.

Selah

    For Sophia

We step out of mourning's song
    like stray notes unsung

and enter the nursery's white
    noise, cool mist, dim light.

Here, as if in secret, we trade
    nourishment. Here we hide

from present and future grief.
    Oh to live in this pause, this relief.

Here, where grace is biochemical,
    and all is right, restored, and well.

Gamâl

>Hebrew for "wean" or "ripen"

Pulling away, she leaves behind the flesh of fruit:
stark black seed of kiwi, blueberry's torn
skin, red jewels of raspberry.
                                  Grape to my vine,
tomato to my garden, she exchanges green
for richer color—softens, brims,
and with her fullness
tugs the stem.
            Slowly, slowly—only
when she stills and quiets,
will I release her,
and she, me.

>Psalm 131:2

Kairos

> New Testament Greek for "the appointed time
> in the purpose of God"

Over, the season of delicate, whirring things,
but the dry domestic air still flutters
with a litany of wings:

Though dead, a dragonfly greeted us
with iridescence on the steps of the beach house.
Its emerald head swiveled in our hands.

A drab moth drowned in the bath,
but twitched, stood, fanned its wings
to our daughter's high-pitched halleluiah.

A monarch flamed from its chrysalis,
met our eyes through jar glass,
then flew from rim toward pines and sky.

Caught in the church, a dragonfly looped
and whirled through the funeral service
like an unburdened spirit.

Now this unexpected conception.
Again, we enter the cocoon of waiting,
which clogs our dreams with fibers of fear.

What of all the autumn caterpillars
our daughter eased into jars, who haven't yet
emerged from their cotton shrouds?

Will there be a resurrection, an unfurling
of new wings? What was—or is—
their appointed time?

Milk Chant

> For Finn

A continent and an ocean away,
I still made milk meant for you.

Faithful to our shared biology,
I expressed it on your schedule.

The cold throats of airport bathroom sinks
swallowed the warm ounces meant for you.

The rich soil of Maui received my richness.
I traced the island, marked my route

with white puddles soaking into red dirt.
Lava rocks bathed in milk meant for you.

I left a broken trail like the bluish stones
that mark the old King's Highway.

I poured lush upon lush, milk sweet as coconuts,
each tidal surge of letdown meant for you—

each small eruption for you but not for you—
the pump hissing your name.

Ars Poetica

I write for the same reason I believe
the Word became flesh: I will die.

Each poem brings me hours
closer to breathlessness, to leaving

a record of words like a line
of mourners. God, forgive my vanity

in wanting remembrance—help me
channel praise to the wellspring.

And if I die while my child
is too young to know me beyond

comforts of face, voice, touch,
may she find me later in lines

rendering what shimmers.
Daughter, perch there with me

like those goldfinches in trees
outside this silver-streaked window

where we sit together,
watching through rain for spring.

Notes on Poems

"Lo & Behold: A Psalm": Psalm 138:3 reads, "In the day when I cried out, You answered me, / And made me bold with strength in my soul."

"Descant on the 23rd Psalm": A sermon by Pastor Ted Justice prompted this poem.

"Doxology with Crow": The epigraph is from Donald Platt's poem "Brother Death, Sister Life" in his collection *My Father Says Grace* (University of Arkansas Press, 2007).

"Red Knot Turning": This poem is in memory of my paternal grandmother, Barbara Wolfe Powlus.

"Barrel": This poem was inspired by Ellen Bryant Voigt's poem "Stone Pond" from her collection *The Lotus Flowers* (W.W. Norton, 1987).

"Aftercare," "Souvenir," and "Cannonball": All three poems are dedicated to my maternal grandmother, Janet Andrus, a poet in her own right.

"Hot Air": This poem was inspired by Tony Hoagland's poem "Cement Truck" from his chapbook *Hard Rain* (Hollyridge Press, 2005).

"Search for Origins": According to NASA.gov, a year after the hard landing of the Genesis, NASA declared the spacecraft's four solar wind collectors to be in surprisingly good shape. After two more years of analysis, researchers disproved a theory that arose from the Apollo lunar missions, which had suggested much higher levels of solar activity billions of years ago. Then in 2011, researcher Kevin McKeegan conveyed the implications of his team's latest findings, saying that the earth and other inner planets, contrary to previous thought, "did not form out of the same solar nebula materials that created the sun—just why remains to be discovered."

"Echolalia": This poem references the children's books *Blueberries for Sal* by Robert McCloskey (The Viking Press, 1948) and *The Creation Story*, illustrated by Norman Messenger (Dorling Kindersley Limited, 2001).

"What is *Near*?": This poem pays tribute to the song "The Nearness of You" by Hoagy Carmichael and Ned Washington.

"*Selah*": This poem is in memory of my father-in-law, Pastor Lynn Allen Wheeler. The Hebrew word *Selah* appears seventy-one times in the Psalms and three times in Habakkuk. Its meaning is unknown and debatable. Some interpret it as a musical term signaling a pause or interlude.

"*Gamâl*": Psalm 131:2 reads, "Surely I have calmed and quieted my soul, / Like a weaned child with his mother; / Like a weaned child is my soul within me."

www.ingramcontent.com/pod-product-compliance
Lightning Source LLC
Chambersburg PA
CBHW070257100426
42743CB00011B/2250